Empowering
Employees

Empowering Employees

L. KRISTI LONG

Business Skills Express Series

IRWIN
Professional Publishing

MIRROR PRESS®
Chicago • Bogotá • Boston • Buenos Aires • Caracas
London • Madrid • Mexico City • Sydney • Toronto

© Richard D. Irwin, a Times Mirror Higher Education Group, Inc. company, 1996

Irwin Professional Book Team

Mirror Press:	*David R. Helmstadter*
	Carla Tishler
Associate publisher:	*Jeffrey A. Krames*
Project editor:	*Beth Cigler*
Production supervisor:	*Pat Frederickson*
Manager, direct marketing:	*Rebecca S. Gordon*
Prepress buyer:	*Jon Christopher*
Designer:	*Matthew Baldwin*
Compositor:	*David Corona Design*
Typeface:	*12/14 ITC Century Book*
Printer:	*Malloy Lithographing, Inc.*

Times Mirror
M Higher Education Group

Library of Congress Cataloging-in-Publication Data

Long, L. Kristi.
    Empowering employees / L. Kristi Long.
        p. cm.— (Business skills express series)
    ISBN 0-7863-0314-X
    1. Employee empowerment. I. Title. II. Series.
    HD50.5.L66 1996
    658.3'14—dc20   95-32042

Printed in the United States of America
  2 3 4 5 6 7 8 9 0 ML 2 1 0 9 8 7

PREFACE

The power of empowerment . . . sounds intriguing doesn't it? More than just a buzzword of the 90s, empowerment can direct management executives, supervisors, and employees to new levels of productivity.

In fact, the effects of employee empowerment on the organization go beyond improved efficiency. As employees assume more control over their work environment and begin to self-direct work efforts, there is an increase in self-confidence and greater self-esteem. Employee empowerment gives workers a sense of ownership.

This book is designed to help you consider the difference between delegation and employee empowerment. It will explain how delegation holds the supervisor responsible for completing the job while employee empowerment shifts the accountability to the employee.

The book will help you determine which employees are suitable for empowerment. It will show you how to develop a job profile for each of the employees you supervise. The profile will help you align the job responsibilities and performance levels necessary for an employee empowerment program to work.

The book will also guide you through the process of putting an employee empowerment program in place. Begin with the self-assessment test to start thinking about empowerment. In each chapter, complete the exercises and evaluate your score. Finally, follow up with skill maintenance to help you stay on track.

A word of advice: Implementing an employee empowerment program is not an overnight job. To develop a successful program, you must be honest about your own abilities and be willing to make a few mistakes. It is never easy to let go. Empowerment is a learning process for supervisors and employees. Your employees must be involved from the very beginning. Employee empowerment is not something you *do to* your employees; it is what you *do with* them. Good luck!

L. Kristi Long

ABOUT THE AUTHOR

L. Kristi Long is director of education for the American Society of Travel Agents. Her extensive background includes positions as a travel counselor and travel agency manager, a tour escort for American Express and Mayflower Tours, vice president of training for Travel Agents International franchise headquarters, and sales director for the Brac Reef Beach Resort and Little Cayman Beach Resort in the Cayman Islands.

Ms. Long has written and presented seminars for North West World Vacations, Ottawa Algonquin Travel, Hickory Travel Systems, American Airlines, Sabre, Sheraton, and Naggar Tours, to name a few. Her specialty topics include employee empowerment, outside sales development, customer service, personal computer skills, and selling techniques.

ABOUT IRWIN PROFESSIONAL PUBLISHING

Irwin Professional Publishing is the nation's premier publisher of business books. As a Times Mirror company, we work closely with Times Mirror training organizations, including Zenger-Miller, Inc., Learning International, Inc., and Kaset International, to serve the training needs of business and industry.

ABOUT THE BUSINESS SKILLS EXPRESS SERIES

This expanding series of authoritative, concise, and fast-paced books delivers high-quality training on key business topics at a remarkably affordable cost. The series will help managers, supervisors, and frontline personnel in organizations of all sizes and types hone their business skills while enhancing job performance and career satisfaction.

Business Skills Express books are ideal for employee seminars, independent self-study, on-the-job training, and classroom-based instruction. Express books are also convenient-to-use references at work.

CONTENTS

Self-Assessment

Take this short test to see if you are a candidate for establishing an employee empowerment program in your company or department.

- Answer each question honestly.
- Answer spontaneously. Don't think too long or too hard about any one question.
- After counting your score, go back and circle the questions you feel are critical to establishing a successful employee empowerment program.

Questions	Almost Always	Sometimes	Almost Never
1. I proof every typed piece of correspondence.	_____	_____	_____
2. I closely monitor my employees' work.	_____	_____	_____
3. For the most part, I am the only one who gets jobs done right the first time.	_____	_____	_____
4. I watch the comings and goings of my employees to ensure that they arrive to work on time, don't take long breaks or lunch hours, and don't leave early.	_____	_____	_____
5. When I see two or more employees talking, I assume they are wasting time.	_____	_____	_____
6. I have more work to do than I can get done.	_____	_____	_____

(Continued)

1 | An Introduction to Empowerment: Is Your Company Ready?

This chapter will help you to: ————————————

- Identify the differences between delegation and empowerment.
- Identify common management methods.
- Describe your business management style.
- Develop an initial definition of empowerment.

Samantha and Frank Stone own Stone Books. The bookstore is located downtown and occupies 700 square feet of a renovated office building. Samantha and Frank have only one employee, a high school student who works after school and on Saturdays.

Samantha is a very organized, meticulous individual who prefers to concentrate on the details side of the business. Frank, on the other hand, has an artistic, creative nature and elects to set up store displays, arrange book signings, and maintain the store's inventory.

Samantha and Frank, however, have not always held defined roles. Early in their business development, they often encountered problems. Stock was double-ordered,

1

or popular books sold out. Three checks bounced within the same month, and twice the store opened late because each partner thought the other was opening the store.

These early difficulties sounded an alarm for the Stones. They sat down and listed the necessary duties involved in running a successful business and divided the responsibilities based on each other's strengths. ■

WHO NEEDS STRUCTURE?

Every business, regardless of size, has management structure. As we saw in the opening vignette, even a small retail outlet operated by a husband-and-wife team with no additional full-time employees has a structure of responsibilities and duties. She keeps the books while he maintains the inventory. She schedules deliveries and he stocks the shelves. Together they decide on store hours, consider a change in location, and monitor their profits and losses.

On the opposite end of the spectrum, very large companies divide operations into divisions. Each division has its own president or, at the very least, an executive vice president overseeing one section of the business. At the very top is the chief executive officer (CEO), integrating divisional presidents into a cohesive and successful organization.

As a company grows, so does the complexity of the organization. Each layer of the hierarchy begins to pile on top of another. Responsibilities and tasks are divided and redivided, and accomplishments are pared back. As this happens, it is easy to lose contact with the people who make up the organization.

Often as companies grow, familiarity with individuals decreases. The person in the mail room or the new entry-level accounting clerk may never be introduced to the president or CEO of a large company and may not even know what he or she looks like except for a portrait hanging in the board room. New-employee orientation is conducted by the personnel department or a supervisor. Upper management is rarely involved.

However, in both small and large companies, getting all workers to "buy in" or make a mental commitment to the business is critical to success. Efforts to include employees in developing policy or making decisions will vary according to management style and philosophy of the company. In many organizations, the way to connect the worker to the company is through delegation of responsibilities, as shown in our first definition of empowerment.

First Definition of Empowerment

Empowerment is the ability to let others assume the responsibilities, risks, and rewards associated with making their own decisions.

DELEGATION AND ITS REWARDS

Delegation, the idea of awarding a task or project to a lower level wage earner, has been a part of business management for quite some time. When managers or supervisors delegate work responsibilities, they free themselves for important tasks while allowing others to feel connected and proud of their contributions to the company.

Successful people will attest to the need to delegate work. Desks piled high with papers, briefcases stuffed to capacity, and work carried home in the evenings and over weekends—all of these cry out for the need to pass along tasks to others.

But is delegating work really the same as passing on responsibility? Are employees inspired to complete the work, and do they feel personal pride when it's done? Do employees consider themselves more valuable to both the company and themselves? Or does delegation simply mean pushing the stress off to someone else, reducing the paperwork on one desk only to increase it on the next?

Delegation Can Lead to Empowerment

Some organizations are taking delegation one step further by empowering their employees. Empowerment differs from delegation in that the control and responsibility for completing the assignment are passed along with the task or project.

Your Turn

Take the following mini quiz to see if you can recognize empowerment. Respond to the five statements by circling T or F.

T F **1.** Most of the decisions made at my place of business are made by top management.

T F **2.** Branch/area managers are never asked for input regarding policy changes.

T F **3.** The company discourages employee suggestions.

T F **4.** When a project fails or a major customer is lost, an individual will bear the blame.

T F **5.** Most interaction between managers and employees involves correcting problems.

Consider the implications of your answers. You might surprise yourself, and you may want to start making an empowerment plan right away.

1. *True*—Your company is not involving its employees in the management of the business. If all decisions are made at the top, middle managers and employees have minimal control and little responsibility for the success of the company.

False—Decision making spread throughout an organization shows trust and confidence in the workforce behind the organization. Employees who have some control in the direction the business takes are more likely to stay with the company.

2. *True*—Middle managers who are rarely asked for input, and who therefore have little say in the running of the business, are not likely to encourage their employees to accept new standards or adjust to procedural changes.

False—Middle managers who are involved in policy making can present new methods or system changes more effectively to their employees.

3. *True*—If suggestions made by employees are never solicited or acted upon, the message sent by management is "You just do your job, and we will take care of everything else."

False—Companies that encourage employee suggestions are more likely to keep employees longer. Everyone likes to feel valued. Acknowledgment or implementation of creative suggestions builds employee confidence and satisfaction.

4. *True*—Organizations that look for a scapegoat to blame are just looking for a quick excuse. Employees and managers are less likely to willingly take on responsibility that may cost them respect or their job.

False—When problems occur, if the company is willing to evaluate the entire situation and take corrective action as a team, more employees will be willing to take risks and participate in various projects.

5. *True*—Employees who are called into the boss's office only to be reprimanded will certainly look for the closest exit when they see the boss coming.

False—Ongoing interaction between managers and employees establishes more confidence in the work environment. Respect and trust are developed only through positive discussions interlaced with suggestions.

Look back at the number of true/false answers that you selected. The *true* responses indicate a top-heavy decision-making organization where most resolutions are made at the senior executive level. *True* answers point toward little employee involvement except when lowering the boom on poor decisions or inappropriate behavior. On the other hand, *false* answers show evidence of a connection between all levels of the workforce. *False* responses imply that an employee voice is heard.

If you answered the quiz with all *true* responses, you have a lot of work to do before creating an employee empowerment program. Management must be willing to loosen the decision-making ropes and let middle managers and their staffs assume more control. Answering the quiz with all *false* answers is an encouraging sign that you are ready for employee empowerment.

TWO COMMON MANAGEMENT MODELS

How, or if, an organization uses *delegation* or *empowerment* depends on its management method. Not every company or manager is suited to establishing an environment that routinely delegates work or empowers employees.

Small to medium companies (with at least 25 people) usually follow the *pyramid* model of organization. In larger conglomerate industries, management is often directed according to the *building blocks* model.

THE PYRAMID MODEL

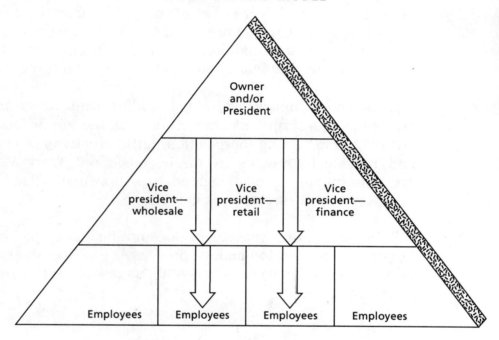

In pyramid companies, the owner or president makes the majority of the decisions. If additional input or guidance is needed, the president solicits the opinion of the vice president in charge of the division the decision will affect. However, final decisions rest with the president.

Decisions made by the president are directed to the vice presidents in charge of various departments, who then relay the information to the employees by bulletin board, memorandum, or staff meeting.

Decisions rarely take into account feedback from front-line employees. Occasionally, a dusty suggestion box is available for strong opinions, but most employees are expected to abide by company policy. Seriously disgruntled employees may quit and move on or will eventually be labeled as troublemakers and be fired.

Rigid pyramid structures may also frustrate vice presidents. With little or no control over policy making, they are forced to ride the company bandwagon yet are faced with delivering unpopular messages. Such an unharmonious situation will create frequent turnovers at the middle management level and within the workforce.

In pyramid frameworks, responsibilities and tasks are strictly layered. Job descriptions are written with the job or task in mind, not the person filling the position. Little creativity is encouraged, and individual strengths are rarely considered. Work assignments are departmentalized, delegated to subordinates, and carefully monitored to ensure correct completion.

This method of management does not enable employees to participate in the decision-making process or to direct their own work efforts. Most employees are seen not as resources or assets, but as replaceable objects.

What's Wrong with This Picture?

Pyramid management does not encourage the entire workforce to "buy in" to the company and its future. In strict pyramid-model companies, it is difficult to get an empowerment program established. The tip of the pyramid is too powerful and often will not relinquish even minor decisions to middle managers. Supervisors are relegated to ensuring that company policy is followed and yield very little influence over setting policy.

In pyramid-model companies, employee morale can be low. Since most decisions are made without their input, many employees begin to feel that the company doesn't care about them as individuals.

Morale, whether positive or negative, determines motivational energy. Positive morale opens the door for recognition of hard work and for the feeling that everyone is an integral part of the organization. Empowerment leads to positive morale.

1

BUILDING BLOCKS MODEL

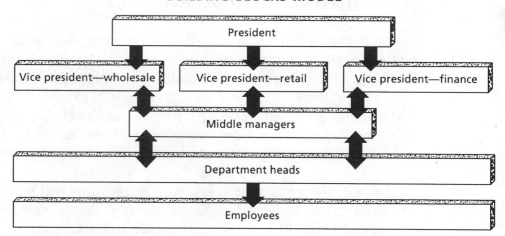

In the building blocks model of management, organizations often separate their management levels into several tiers. As in the pyramid model, policy flows down from the top. However, middle management is allowed more responsibility than in the pyramid model. Middle managers often control daily procedures and focus on getting company goals completed. Senior management's objectives are to set those goals and decide the course of affairs for the entire company.

Regularly scheduled meetings are held with senior executives and the chief executive officer and/or president. Senior executives in turn convene middle managers and department heads, who focus on topics specific to their areas. Middle managers can assemble task forces or committees to resolve specific issues. Not every committee decision makes a long-term mark, however.

If executed correctly, building block management can get the total workforce involved in operating the company. The opportunity to participate at even a small level gives employees a sense of control and self-direction, leading to better morale and therefore improved productivity.

BUILDING EMPOWERMENT

In the building blocks model of management, decisions are based on the information gathered from the various layers of management. Each layer provides input collected from every area of the company.

It sounds good. However, problems can develop when multiple opinions and theories from every level of management muddy the waters and turn simple decisions into complicated resolutions.

Also, consider that not everyone's suggestion will be included in the final draft. Rejected suggestions may create rejected middle managers who will be less enthusiastic to participate next time. A negative reaction can be infectious and, if widespread, can cripple a business.

Even with these negatives, building block management is better suited for delegation and employee empowerment, since it relies on a two-way flow of information. Getting input from various levels of the organization is seen as an important step toward making major decisions. All that remains is to let some of the control rest in the lower layers of the company.

For employee empowerment to work, management must let selected employees assume control of a given task and take it to completion.

Defining Empowerment

As you have discovered in this chapter, delegation and empowerment differ in the degree of control and responsibility assumed by the employee. Not every organization or supervisor is a candidate for initiating an employee empowerment plan. To see if you are developing a better understanding of employee empowerment, take a minute to write your own definition:

1

Employee empowerment is

_____

_____

_____

_____

Before moving to Chapter 2, take a minute to think back on the Stones in our opening vignette. They were able to determine what was keeping them from growing their business and to make the necessary changes. Despite being such a small organization, they were able to initiate the structure necessary to ensure a successful operation. Each partner assumed responsibilities, and both were empowered to make the decisions relative to their accountable areas.

■ Think about It

In the exercise below, list the areas of responsibility that fall under your direction. After completing the list, carefully consider each area and mark off any that might be passed on to a selected employee to assume control and completion. The first two are done as examples.

Area of Responsibility	Pass It On
Weekly work schedule	X
Annual budget	

✔ Delegation and empowerment differ in the degree of responsibility given to employees.

✔ A company's use of delegation or empowerment depends on its management model: pyramid, building blocks, or in-between.

✔ Employee empowerment is not suited to rigid top management control.

✔ The responsibility for empowering employees rests on primary supervisors and middle managers.

2 | Can Every Employee be Empowered?

This chapter will help you to:

- Identify obstacles that create barriers to empowerment.
- Create a job profile for each employee who is a candidate for empowerment.
- Understand the three primary communication differences that may surface between supervisors and employees.
- Set standards for an empowerment program.
- Examine the importance of feedback in developing a successful empowerment program.

Clarence Willis is seriously considering initiating an employee empowerment program. He feels that each member of his staff has the ability to make independent decisions and that most have the necessary skills to assume more responsibility for their own work projects.

Clarence jots down a few notes as his mind balances the possibilities. He writes:

- Can I let go?
- Am I at risk? Are they at risk?
- Should everyone be included?
- Who would I select if I started with only one or two?
- Empowerment would give me more time.
- Empowerment would open the door for increased pride and self-esteem.

Clarence lists each employee and gives each name careful consideration. He marks a small asterisk beside five names and decides to make an appointment with each of these employees to discuss the idea of empowerment. ■

Every employee is essentially his or her own manager. Individually, each chooses his or her own work effort, team participation, and overall energy output. No one can force someone else to display and maintain any particular level of effort. Management can provide a resource for encouragement, feedback, and reinforcement, but only the employee can select how much control and responsibility he or she is willing to take on.

OBSTACLES TO EMPOWERMENT

Three common obstacles to empowering employees are ambition, overmanagement, and poor job profiles. These obstacles can be overcome if recognized by the employee, the supervisor, or both. The following table outlines these obstacles and offers guidelines for overcoming them.

Obstacle	Supervisor	Employee
Ambition	Supervisors who believe they must maintain a superior position over their employees are often reluctant to empower staff for fear that ambitious employees will rise above them or get promoted faster than they will.	Employees may believe that assuming an empowered position may make them appear overly ambitious and may threaten their supervisor. Job security may take precedence over ambition. They may also feel concern over how their peers will react if they appear too ambitious.

(Continued)

2

Overcoming the Obstacle

Empowering employees offers the opportunity to get more accomplished. Getting more done will only increase the supervisor's worth to the company.	Taking on more control and responsibility allows every level of employee to increase productivity. Ambition is equated with energy and enthusiasm, not overzealous climbing of the corporate ladder.

Obstacle	Supervisor	Employee
Overmanagement	Control is difficult to relinquish. Micromanaging employees creates a limited step-by-step work environment where employees wait for the next step or instruction before proceeding.	Employees who get used to being directed at every level of output will often slow their work effort until the next instruction is given. Overmanagement reduces individual initiative and blankets self-confidence.

Overcoming the Obstacle

Loosening control does not come without risk and reward. Supporting employees while increasing their responsibilities will increase productivity and develop each employee's potential.	Employees may not initially welcome added responsibility and increased control over their work projects. However, empowerment will enhance self-esteem and develop higher attitudes of self-worth.

Obstacle	Supervisor	Employee
Poor job profile	Employee empowerment will require updating or rewriting current job descriptions. Misunderstandings are bound to surface without a clear guide for new responsibilities. Make sure to define new position structures and personal requirements.	Employees will not greet empowerment with enthusiasm if they are unsure of expectations. Lack of clear guidelines will create confusion and problems. All empowered employees must understand their new role and their new capabilities.

Overcoming the Obstacle

Job profiles for each empowered position should include technical job skills and performance skills. Technical job skills are observable and measurable activities necessary to complete the job. Performance skills relate more to work habits such as creativity, flexibility, and sociability. A job profile completed for each position will provide a clear guide for expected work performance.	Empowered employees should have some input in the rewriting of their job profile. The process of redefining their work responsibilities will encourage exploration into new standards and clarify the involvement necessary to to implement the new job profile. The redesigned description will give new perspective on job duties.

2

CREATING A JOB PROFILE

A job profile should be completed on each person participating in an employee empowerment program. To develop job profiles for your employees, consider each person individually. For each, fill in the worksheet on page 19. By completing individual worksheets, you will be forced to look at each staff member and evaluate his or her current level of skills, and to determine where improvements are needed. Adapt the job profile worksheet as needed to fit the jobs in your company.

In order to make an empowerment program effective, careful consideration must be given to job standards, responsibility factors, and performance levels.

Job Profile Worksheet

Employee Name: _____ Position/Title: _____

For each employee, write *H* for High, *M* for Medium, and *L* for Low to indicate the degree to which the employee has obtained the listed skills.

Job Skill	Current Level (H-M-L)	Optimum Level (H-M-L)	Suggested Improvements
Technical knowledge	_____	_____	_____
Work quality	_____	_____	_____
Specialized skills	_____	_____	_____
Analytical skills	_____	_____	_____
Customer contact	_____	_____	_____
Vendor contact	_____	_____	_____
Appearance	_____	_____	_____
Energy level	_____	_____	_____
Creative thinking	_____	_____	_____
Personal judgment	_____	_____	_____
Adapts to change	_____	_____	_____
Can handle pressure	_____	_____	_____
Makes independent decisions	_____	_____	_____
Positive attitude about company	_____	_____	_____
Relationship with co-workers	_____	_____	_____
Relationship with supervisor	_____	_____	_____
Reliability	_____	_____	_____
Ability to communicate	_____	_____	_____
Cooperativeness	_____	_____	_____
Self-confidence	_____	_____	_____
Organizational skills	_____	_____	_____

2

2

Only you can determine which skills are necessary for an employee empowerment plan to work for both the employee and the organization. Important to the success of any new management strategy is preparing the workers who must carry out the program. By pre-evaluating skill levels, you can first improve weak areas for each employee. By developing individual skills, you will better position the employee to succeed in empowerment.

IDENTIFYING DIFFERENCES

Since every employee is essentially his or her own manager with or without empowerment, how can you identify differences that may go unspoken? The basis for empowerment has to be communication. Effective communication will go far in overcoming employee differences in expectations of what empowerment will entail.

Employees will also have different objectives and different methods for handling empowerment. Communication can bridge the differences so that everyone comes closer to a full-scale commitment to empowerment.

Differences in Objectives. The objective of an empowerment program is to move toward a more autonomous work environment where independent decisions are blended with a willingness to work together to achieve company goals. Supervisors must learn to support without removing responsibility. Employees must be willing to take on risk and to challenge the institutionalized process of being told what to do.

Differences in Assumptions. Assumptions, which are internal conversations with ourselves, place a heavy burden on communication. It is easy to assume that everyone understands your expectations. It is equally easy to assume that everyone has the same understanding of the same situation. A successful employee empowerment program is never based on assumptions. Clear and concise

2

communication, where each side understands the objectives and goals of the organization, is critical.

Differences in Methods.　The very concept of empowerment is based on individual choice. The actual method of completing an assignment takes a back seat to the end result. When a project is assigned to an empowered employee, the three following key elements must be understood fully by both the supervisor and the employee:

1. The project to be completed.
2. What is expected.
3. The completion date.

For supervisors, a difficult area to overcome in establishing an employee empowerment program is to let go of how a task gets done and instead concentrate on the end result. Just because an employee does not stack papers the same way you do doesn't mean he or she is disorganized.

Your Turn: Letting Go

Are you able to let go enough to make employees feel empowered? Answer the following questions quickly. Choose the first response that comes to mind. Mark an *A* if the statement or question *always* applies to you. Mark an *S* if the statement or question *sometimes* applies to you. Mark an *N* if the statement *never* applies to you.

_____　　**1.** It is usually easier to do something myself than to assign it.

_____　　**2.** Explaining the details of a project is too time-consuming. I prefer to give only enough information to get the work done.

_____　　**3.** It drives me crazy when I don't know every detail of a project.

2

_____   **4.** A messy desk is a sure sign of a disorganized person.

_____   **5.** When an employee makes a mistake, I find it hard to trust that person again.

_____   **6.** No one does a better job than I do.

_____   **7.** Employees are like children. You can't take your eyes off them for a second.

_____   **8.** I feel threatened if an employee pushes for more responsibility.

_____   **9.** I really don't care if my staff likes me.

_____   **10.** I'm going to give directions only once. If someone doesn't grasp what is supposed to be done, tough.

Scoring:

For every _A_ give yourself two points; for every _S_ give yourself one point.

Scores of 15 or higher indicate that you are rather autocratic in your management style. It is more difficult for autocratic supervisors to establish an empowerment program. By nature, autocrats tend to be controlling and practically demand to be in on every decision. It might be best for high scorers to start slowly with an empowerment program. Start with one or two staff members on projects that are to be completed in less than six months. Set standards for the project with the input from the selected staff and allow for plenty of feedback as you proceed. The combination of only one or two employees, agreed-upon standards, and consistent feedback will offer you a comfortable environment in which you can begin to let go and open the door for employees to assume more responsibility.

(Continued)

> If you scored 14 or less, it will be easier for you to establish an employee empowerment program. Your score indicates that you are less controlling and are more likely to let employees assume greater responsibility for their own job efforts. However, the necessary steps of setting standards and gathering feedback apply as well.

2

As you can see from the quiz, it is crucial to set standards and gather feedback. An empowerment program cannot be sustained without the following key elements:

KEY ELEMENTS

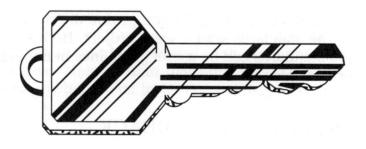

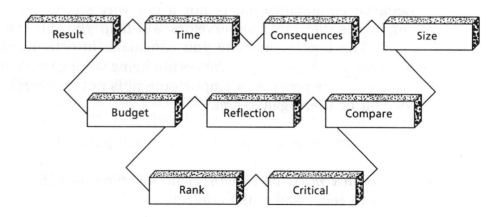

Result   Time   Consequences   Size

Budget   Reflection   Compare

Rank   Critical

2

1. You have empowered an employee to develop the weekly work schedules. The initial effort has created serious shortages during two shifts and a barrage of complaints. Role-play a conversation between the scheduler and a shift worker who does not like his or her schedule.

2. The education committee for your association is planning to meet in April. You have assigned the meeting to one of your employees, who is to find a meeting location, coordinate the attendees, and arrange travel with the company travel agent. Role-play your initial discussion with the employee. (Make sure the role play includes the key standards.)

3. Select two potential empowerment candidates for the role play. Create a pretend situation where you have selected one of them to develop and implement a new office policy manual. The employee not selected is asked to assist in the development at the request of the empowered employee. Role-play the exchange between the selected employee and the somewhat disgruntled employee who was not selected as the first asks the second for his or her assistance.

After each role play, spend time evaluating the exchange. Let the role-play participants comment on their own "performance" and what they have learned. Remember the guidelines for offering feedback. Keep the situation positive and balanced. Be objective and don't mix your personal opinions with the specifics of the role play.

Your hardest challenge will be getting the participants to relax and have fun with the role play. Let the role play flow naturally, but put a time cap on each example. Lengthy role play will stray from the topic and will make extracting specific points difficult.

Chapter 2
Checkpoints

✔ Every employee is essentially his or her own manager. Give careful consideration to the common obstacles that may create barriers to empowering employees.

✔ Create a job profile for each employee to allow you to evaluate employees' skill levels before they are selected for an empowerment program. Skills that are critical to empowerment can be improved before you initiate your program.

✔ Understand that differences in *objectives*, in *assumptions*, and in *methods* need to be overcome if both the supervisor and the employee are to communicate on the same wavelength.

✔ Develop key standards for the empowerment project and consider matching the job profile to the standards set.

3 | Employee Motivation

This chapter will help you to:

- Explore traditional employee motivation.
- Examine the effects of job environment and job content on work performance.
- Identify extrinsic and intrinsic characteristics functioning within the job environment.
- Determine what motivates your staff.

Kim Sung has worked for The Music Makers for five years. At each annual employee evaluation, Kim has been offered a pay increase ranging from 4 percent to 10 percent and at year 4 gained a second week's vacation. In addition, Kim's title has been upgraded from research assistant to lead researcher.

At the start of his employment with The Music Makers, Kim Sung was a model employee. He arrived early, stayed late, never required sick leave, and never asked for additional time off. Lately, however, Kim is showing signs of discontent with his job. He arrives late at least once a week, rarely stays past 5 PM, and almost routinely calls in sick once every three months. Kim has missed important project deadlines twice in the last three months.

Karen Wallace, Kim's supervisor, is beginning to think that it is time to replace Kim. After all, the company has given him pay raises and a better title, so what else could Kim expect? Karen has recorded a note in Kim's personnel file that reads, "Work effort is diminishing along with employee's attitude. Will monitor for the next three months and reevaluate." ■

IS MONEY THE ONLY MOTIVATOR?

What is happening to Kim Sung and Karen Wallace in the opening vignette is not uncommon in the work arena. Kim Sung's initial job expectations have changed. When he first came on board with The Music Makers, he concentrated on the potential salary, the benefits package, and his overall first impression of the company. As time passed, these issues became routine and were no longer motivating Kim to stay productive and active in the company.

On management's side, Karen Wallace has fallen victim to a common misunderstanding. Karen made the assumption that as long as her employees got annual pay increases and an occasional benefits perk, they would continue to be the same enthusiastic and eager employees who were originally hired.

The primary problem behind this dilemma is the expectation that money is the motivating factor for employees. Unfortunately, that assumption is incorrect. Don't misunderstand, money is important; however, it is not the most important factor when it comes to worker satisfaction, longevity, and productivity. Empowerment plays an important motivating role.

Organizations successful at employee empowerment realize that compensating the worker with a salary and fringe benefits is no guarantee that the worker will be motivated to work above just doing the job. As we will see later in this book, successful employee empowerment programs demonstrate an understanding of the differences between job environment factors and job content motivators. In Kim's case, there doesn't seem to be any motivators in the content of the job—and this is directly related to empowerment.

Let's step back for a moment and look at human motivation in general and at worker motivation specifically. Several famous studies have dominated the material available on this topic, but the two that stand out are Abraham Maslow's "hierarchy of needs" theory and Frederick Herzberg's "intrinsic and extrinsic factors" theory.

Maslow's Hierarchy of Needs

3

In 1954, Abraham Maslow suggested that human needs were arranged in a series of levels or stages. Each level in the hierarchy had to be conquered before an individual could move up to the next. At the very bottom were the *basic needs* of food, shelter, and sleep. Maslow surmised that when a person had the basics for surviving he or she moved up a level to *safety needs*. Once on the second level, if a person felt assured of protection from injury or harm, he or she rose to the third level, that of *social needs* (belonging and feeling loved). At this third level, acceptance and affection gave rise to yet a fourth stage, defined as *esteem needs*. Esteem needs were characterized as feelings of self-worth, self-respect, and status. At the final level, the very top rung in the ladder consisted of *self-actualization needs*. This last step brought the realization of potentialities and an expression of personal growth.

According to Maslow's theory, as needs were met at each level, an individual would turn his or her attention to the next higher level. Self-actualization was the ultimate achievement.

Herzberg's Extrinsic and Intrinsic Factors

In the mid-1960s, Frederick Herzberg put forth a theory on worker motivation in which multiple factors were found to contribute to job satisfaction and to cause job dissatisfaction. He isolated two categories of factors, *extrinsic* and *intrinsic*.

3

Extrinsic factors come from the job itself and include such areas as salary, benefits, and working conditions. Herzberg believed that extrinsic factors could create a feeling of dissatisfaction with a job or could at best bring worker satisfaction to a neutral level (neither satisfactory nor dissatisfactory). They could not promote motivation. In the opening vignette, Kim's factors (pay and benefits) were only extrinsic.

On the other hand, intrinsic factors come from within the work and relate to the worker's perception of achievement, recognition, and advancement. For Herzberg, it was this second category that was the basis for employee motivation. Job satisfaction resulted when employees utilized their skills and perceived themselves as making a contribution to the company. If their efforts were recognized and the opportunity for advancement was offered, the workers' overall satisfaction with the job increased.

According to Herzberg, it is possible for a worker to be dissatisfied and satisfied at the same time. For example, an employee can be disgruntled over the company policy relating to vacation leave, but genuinely satisfied with his or her work performance when a complimentary letter from a customer is posted on the bulletin board in the employee lounge.

ARE NEEDS INTRINSIC OR EXTRINSIC?

For Herzberg, identifying both intrinsic and extrinsic factors was the basis for defining employee motivation. He recognized that every employee would have a different life situation and his or her own set of priorities, but he was convinced that money alone was not the primary reason workers stayed with one company over a period of time.

For an empowerment program to work effectively, both factors weigh into the success. The extrinsic job factors specific to your employees must not be dissatisfying. The salary and benefits package must be in the average range for the industry and for your organization. Working conditions should be comfortable, and employees must feel safe and secure while on the job. (Remember, Maslow proposed that safety needs were relatively basic in the hierarchy leading to self-actualization.) If the extrinsic factors are at a satisfactory level, a well-planned empowerment program will activate the intrinsic side of your employees. Empowered employees perceive their contribution to the job and the organization at a higher level. Add recognition from management and from peers, along with an opportunity for advancement, and you have a productive and motivated workforce. Our second definition of empowerment takes these factors into account.

Second Definition of Empowerment

Employee empowerment is an organization-initiated program that meets the extrinsic needs of employees while building on the intrinsic factors important to job satisfaction and the success of both the worker and the organization.

Think about It

Take a minute to complete the following checklist. Mark an *E* if you identify the item as an extrinsic factor and an *I* if you think it is an intrinsic factor. Recognizing the difference will assist you in determining what areas may be functioning as dissatisfiers or satisfiers for your employees.

☐ Designated parking slots   ☐ Health insurance
☐ Production summary   ☐ A handshake
☐ A two-week vacation   ☐ Service awards
☐ Profit sharing plan   ☐ A new title
☐ Employee evaluation   ☐ A letter from the company president
☐ A job description   ☐ A raise in pay

How do you think you did? The extrinsic factors, those relating to the job itself, are *designated parking slots, health insurance, production summary, a two-week vacation, profit sharing plan, employee evaluation, a raise in pay,* and *a job description.* The remaining are intrinsic factors.

Now that you have a better understanding of Herzberg's two categories, develop a list of your own. First, list the extrinsic factors relating to your company or business. Second, list the intrinsic factors that may be coming into play. The lists do not have to have an equal number of entries.

Extrinsic	Intrinsic

CONTENT VERSUS ENVIRONMENT

Look again at the list in the preceding exercise. Notice that the extrinsic factors fall into job environment while the intrinsic factors cover job content. In order to implement a successful employee empowerment program, you must make sure that the job environment expectations (extrinsic factors) are being met. If the working conditions are poor and the compensation below average, you will have a tough time accenting the job content motivational areas (intrinsic factors).

Employee empowerment's success relies heavily on the job content factors of achievement, recognition, the work itself, responsibility, advancement, and growth/learning. The very essence of empowerment is encouraging staff members to assume greater control of their own work effort, making decisions, and staying with the tough problems or projects through completion.

In the beginning stages of an empowerment program, you may choose to select one or two employees or one department to get started. It will be easier to consider intrinsic versus extrinsic factors and job content versus job environment areas on a small basis before applying empowerment to the entire organization.

Let's look at job environment versus job content more closely.

JOB ENVIRONMENT

Policy	Responsibility	Working Conditions
Manager/ Employee Relations		Peer Relations

Environment

Achievement	Recognition	Work
Responsibility	Advancement	Growth

Content

Job Environment

When a person first interviews for a new job, job environment factors play an important role in the decision to take the job. *How much money will I make? How many vacation days will I get? Where will my office be located?* These are the questions the job interviewee thinks about, even if he or she doesn't voice them.

The five main facets of *job environment* are:

1. Policy and administration
   Hiring
   Firing
   Grievance procedures
   Overtime
   Compensatory time
   Sick leave/funeral leave
   Holiday closings
   Work rules (dress code, breaks, smoking, desks, etc.)

2. Compensation
   Salary
   Commissions
   Bonuses
   Health insurance
   Vacation leave

3. Working conditions
   Space and layout
   Noise
   Lighting
   Furnishings
   General atmosphere

4. Manager/employee relations
   Fair scheduling
   Equitable assignments
   Clear instructions
   Impartial employee evaluations

5. Peer relations
   Teamwork
   Outside activities (bowling league, softball team, etc.)
   Moderate competition
   Proportionate workloads

When hiring new employees, supervisors often focus on job environment factors, since these tend to attract good employees (if these factors are top level and competitive with other companies' benefits) and keep good employees. Recruiting, interviewing, and training new hires is expensive in both time and money. Maintaining a good job environment is crucial to avoiding a constant cycle of employee turnover, which can be detrimental to a company's success, not to mention its survival.

Job Content

Employee empowerment goes one step further than providing an attractive work environment. Empowerment addresses the job content sector, along with the employee's emotions and perceptions of the work itself. In other words, in a company where employee empowerment is practiced, supervisors enhance the quality of the work experience (the content) rather than only the trappings (the environment).

The six aspects of job content are:

1. Achievement
   Utilizing skills
   Making a contribution
   Meeting objectives
   Developing new programs, services, products
2. Recognition
   Written or verbal commendation
   Monetary bonus
   A gift, a dinner certificate, theater tickets, etc.
   A handshake or pat on the back

3 Work itself
   Challenging assignments
   Special projects
   Developing specific job interests

4. Responsibility
   Sharing in the company's performance goals
   Freedom to prioritize work demands
   Authority to get the job done
   Monitoring personal workmanship

5. Advancement
   Recognized promotion
   Increased wages and benefits
   Prestigious office location
   Reserved parking space
   Key to the executive washroom

6. Growth/learning
   In-house training
   Adult education courses
   Conferences/seminars

DIVERSITY MAKES A DIFFERENCE

How can you create one motivation system that suits a diverse workforce? If all employees had like interests and goals, and were stimulated by the same factors, management could easily create an employee motivation plan.

Of course, it is not that simple. Employees who seem quite similar may have markedly different work performances. Consider the following example.

Rachel Rosenburg joined The Music Makers one month after Kim Sung. She too was hired as a research assistant and after five years still holds that title. Like Kim Sung, Rachel has received annual salary increases and an extra week's vacation.

About a year after Rachel came to The Music Makers, Karen Wallace noticed Rachel's enthusiasm for classical artists. Karen was pleased to hear that Rachel had enrolled in a classical composers class at the local college. When Rachel won Employee of the Month, Karen selected two box-seat tickets to a special concert featuring baroque music as Rachel's award.

Rachel does not know it yet, but she has been selected to head a new research division. The announcement about the new classical music department and Rachel's promotion will come at next month's company picnic. Rachel will be given the opportunity to select her own staff, one lead researcher and four assistant researchers from within the staff of The Music Makers. Developing a profitable classical music sector for The Music Makers will be Rachel's new responsibility. ■

Kim Sung and Rachel Rosenburg seem to have started on the same track, but they have gone separate ways. They both have had the same supervisor, Karen Wallace, and the same opportunities to advance. However, like all employees, Kim and Rachel have different priorities, interests, dislikes, and expectations.

Your Turn: Determining Employee Motivation

In choosing candidates for an employee empowerment program, it is important to recognize individual differences and to discover what motivates each employee.

Give your staff members the following list. Instruct them to circle the five items they would consider inspiring or motivating to perform well. Add any items you consider pertinent to your employees' work environment.

1. The opportunity for promotion.
2. Getting along well with others at work.

3. Freedom from stress.
4. Fair treatment of everybody.
5. People contact.
6. Steady employment and pension benefits.
7. Working for an efficient, organized boss.
8. Increased control over my job.
9. Being told by the boss that I do a good job.
10. Tasks that challenge me.
11. Feeling my job is important.
12. The chance to do quality work.
13. Knowing exactly what is expected from me.
14. Teamwork and cooperation within the office.
15. Respect for me as a person and appreciation of my efforts.

There are no right or wrong answers. However, certain selections on the list point toward needed employee empowerment characteristics. Employees selecting items 3, 9, and 13 are not ideal candidates. Empowerment adds to the responsibilities of employees and requires independent decisions. Employees who indicate a desire for freedom from stress, being told they are doing a good job, and knowing exactly what is expected from them may not be ready for employee empowerment.

On the other hand, if your staff members circled 8, 10, 12, and 14, empowerment may fit well into their work activities. Employee empowerment creates added control for employees and opens the way for greater challenges. For employees to be good candidates for an employee empowerment program that will benefit the employee and the company, empowered team members must demand a high quality of work for themselves. They must also see teamwork and cooperation as needed ingredients to ensure an overall productive organization.

As you make your decision to engage in an employee empowerment program, it is important to consider the job factors that affect each employee and to understand how each factor can potentially dissatisfy, satisfy, or motivate workers. Not every employee will be stimulated by the same circumstances.

Chapter 3
Checkpoints

✔ Money is not the primary factor motivating employees.

✔ Everyone wants to reach a level of self-actualization, but basic needs must be met first.

✔ Extrinsic job factors are at best a neutral satisfier and can be powerful dissatisfiers.

✔ Supervisors must identify the intrinsic job factors and measure which ones are important to their employees.

4 | How to Introduce an Empowerment Plan at Your Company

This chapter will help you to:

- Take the first step toward establishing an employee empowerment plan.
- Identify possible employee reactions.
- Complete an employee assessment for each person under your direction.

Rumor has it at Perfect Printing that management is about to introduce new employee procedures. Top executives and first-level supervisors have been meeting for several weeks. No one is specifically talking about the content of these meetings, but enough comments have come out to start the rumor mill churning. The employees have begun talking among themselves, and most are expecting the worst. They are concerned about their jobs and are becoming increasingly anxious about a heavier workload. So much time is being spent discussing the uncertain possibilities that production is decreasing and some deadlines are not being met. ■

As we saw in Chapter 1, management's views toward implementing employee empowerment will vary according to management theory and philosophy. The decision to empower employees with additional responsibilities, however, is only half the formula. The second and equally important ingredient is assessing the reaction and gaining the support of the employees themselves.

For empowerment to work, managers must:

- Thoroughly explain the concept.
- Assure employees that mistakes will not jeopardize their jobs.
- Select the right employee "test" group in a pilot program.
- Carefully consider which projects or tasks will be directed to employee control.

HANDLING EMPLOYEE REACTIONS

Initially, all employees will not be enthusiastic about assuming additional responsibilities. Supervisors should expect many reactions and varying levels of acceptance. Some employees will respond with:

Suspicion—Some employees may doubt that management is sincere about letting them assume more control over decisions.

Fear—Some employees may worry that empowerment is merely a plan to rid the company of poor decision makers.

Displeasure—If employees have witnessed previous attempts by management to instill a pride-in-performance philosophy, employee empowerment may be viewed as another misguided endeavor.

Overenthusiasm—Some employees may expect to take total control of all decisions relating to their work area and may want to direct all of their own efforts.

These and other reactions can easily be addressed if management takes the time to explain the empowerment program and spends additional time with concerned individual employees. By observing the initial reactions to employee empowerment, managers will be able to read employees' body language and eye movement. When you deliver news of your empowerment plan, watch for arms crossed over the chest, side glances at other employees, closed eyes, eyes directed downward, chins resting on the palm of the hand, and even obvious head shaking.

Management must resist the urge to discount negative employees or exclude them from the program. For employee empowerment to be successful, it is critical that contrary reactions are acknowledged and discussed. By eliciting the opinions of the less enthusiastic, managers will reassure employees that they are valuable to the company and that employee empowerment is a sincere companywide goal.

For some positive and negative reactions to common employee misgivings, consider the following examples.

KEVIN: *We've heard this all before. How is this new empowerment plan any different?*

Poor Response: Don't be ridiculous. This company has never had an employee empowerment plan. Why would you even say that?

Good Response: I realize that other employee involvement ideas have been tried in the past and have not met with great success. This new program teams supervisors and staff as a cohesive unit. With your support, we can make it work.

CASSANDRA: *My workload is overwhelming now. Will this program add to my current duties?*

Poor Response: Everybody in this company thinks they are overworked and underpaid. You could handle more work if you set better priorities.

Good Response: I'm sure a lot of us feel overburdened at times. Some of our work mounts up because management decisions are occasionally slow in coming. With employee empowerment, you will be empowered to make some of these decisions. Therefore, more work can be completed sooner.

4

◼ Your Turn

Write a poor response and a good response to the employee reaction given below.

BETH: *How soon will the entire plan be in writing so we can see the details in black and white?*

Poor Response: _____
_____
_____
_____

Good Response: _____
_____
_____
_____

Write a good response that improves on the poor response given in the next example.

RASHIM: *Is this a volunteer setup, or are you telling us that everyone is going to participate?*

Poor Response: In the first phase, only about a third of the employee base will be selected. The choices

will be based on job descriptions that we
have decided best fit into an empowerment
plan. Volunteering has nothing to do with it.

Good Response: _____
_____
_____
_____

In completing good and poor responses in the above exercise, you
can begin to understand how critical explaining the initial concept
of employee empowerment and responding to employees' questions
is to the outcome of the program. The words and attitudes demon-
strated by management set the tone for any empowerment plan.
Enthusiasm, confidence, and trust must flow down from the executive level to the plant floor.

STEP 1: INTRODUCTION

Supervisors and middle managers who want their employees more
involved in decision making must be ready to coach them on how
to proceed. Your first move toward implementing employee empowerment can lay a solid foundation or a weak one.

In deciding how to take the first step, be creative. Think like an
employee, not a manager. Don't lose that perspective if you want
your group to react positively.

Consider the following strategies:

1. *Establish a task force or committee.* Employees who can
participate in making decisions or building company policy will
be more understanding of management's reasoning behind certain judgments. Everyone likes to feel important and valuable.
Asking for their assistance and opinions will ensure a program
they feel a part of, instead of one that is forced on them.

2. *Hire an outside consultant or speaker.* During work hours, hold a meeting that everyone can attend. Depending on the type of business, it may be necessary to stagger the attendance or conduct two or more meetings. Do not mandate a before-work or after-work assembly. This only throws a negative cloud over the program and relays the message that what is about to come is another enforced procedure or policy.

Bringing in an outside speaker will create a sense of importance about the meeting. Hire a motivational speaker who can transmit an exciting message regarding self-direction, pride in performance, and the power of control. Inform the group that program details will be outlined in a memo from the president and that questions and suggestions will be encouraged. Supervisors and managers should set aside time for discussions with their employee groups.

3. *Conduct an employee rally.* Hold a special staff meeting with a festive atmosphere to encourage camaraderie and team spirit among your staff. Announce the employee empowerment initiative, but keep the message light and fun. Details can be provided later in writing or during individual or small group discussions.

4. *Meet with individual employees or small groups.* Supervisors can arrange short appointments to explain the program to individual employees if the workforce is small, or to groups of three or four if larger numbers are involved.

Group the appointments closely together in order to get the information out quickly. If meetings are spread over several days, the internal grapevine will take over and the risk of misinformation or misunderstanding runs high.

Allow sufficient time for questions, comments, or suggestions. Try to keep each meeting about the same length. If one lasts 15 minutes and one lasts 35 minutes, the first person or group will think the second group was told more.

Listen to what each employee thinks. You cannot force empowerment on people. Be reassuring, enthusiastic, and encouraging.

STEP 2: MAKING CHOICES

Before deciding to establish an employee empowerment program, take a minute to consider each employee and whether he or she will assume the responsibility favorably or perhaps should not be included.

Tip

Not every employee within the company is a candidate for employee empowerment. While most job descriptions or duties lend themselves to some level of individual control, the job and personal qualities must complement each other to make empowerment possible.

Job Areas Suitable for Empowerment Programs:

Customer service	Sales
Accounting	Purchasing
Shipping	Delivery
Reception	Quality control
Production	

 Think about It

You may want to complete the employee assessment form on page 50 for each person you supervise. As you do the exercise, remember to:

- Answer each question honestly.
- Answer spontaneously. Don't think too long or too hard about any one question.

After rating each employee, circle questions relating to areas of potential employee improvement and begin developing individual plans to help these employees (and your organization) get the most out of employee empowerment.

Employee Name: _____

	Always	Sometimes	Never
1. Shows enthusiasm toward the company.	_____	_____	_____
2. Completes work assignments on a timely basis.	_____	_____	_____
3. Arrives to work on time.	_____	_____	_____
4. Stays overtime to complete projects.	_____	_____	_____
5. Can handle deadline pressure or stress.	_____	_____	_____
6. Makes few errors.	_____	_____	_____
7. Understands assignments the first time. Additional instruction is usually not required.	_____	_____	_____
8. Has the ability to prioritize multiple projects.	_____	_____	_____
9. Likes new assignments.	_____	_____	_____
10. Has the ability to work independently.	_____	_____	_____

Scoring

Count the number of Always, Sometimes, and Never answers. Multiply the Always answers by 3. Multiply the Sometimes answers by 2, and let the Never responses count as 1.

30–24   This employee is an excellent candidate for empowerment since he or she already demonstrates work habits and personal characteristics appropriate for empowered workers. Knowing how to set priorities, work independently, and see jobs through to completion are excellent signs of an employee ready for empowerment.

23–16   Employees scoring in the middle range show promise toward developing into qualified empowered employees. This group will need monitoring and coaching to gain the experience and confidence needed for empowered decisions. Begin by delegating short assignments, and rescore in three to six months.

15–10   Scores in this range indicate an employee who needs tight supervision and frequent correction. You are probably spending (and wasting) too much time on keeping track of a worker at this level. Consider replacing this worker.

4

Chapter 4
Checkpoints

✔ Give careful consideration to how employee empowerment will be introduced.

✔ Consider the possible initial reactions that may surface.

✔ Write down possible comments that employees may make and write effective responses that focus on the positive benefits of empowerment.

✔ Evaluate the strengths and weaknesses of each of your employees to help you see if an empowerment program is appropriate for your staff.

5 | Making Empowerment Work

This chapter will help you to: ─────────

- Recognize the importance of companywide commitment to employee empowerment.
- Identify the six key issues for management in implementing an employee empowerment plan.
- Consider which type of manager you are in each of the six management areas.

Linda Pippen has worked for Blackwells Boutique for three years. One day as she walked from the staff locker room to her position in ladies' blouses, she noticed a customer looking through several racks of merchandise. Linda asked if she could be of assistance. The customer responded with "I hope so" and handed Linda a blouse. Linda noticed that the blouse had been worn and probably laundered several times. The customer began to tell Linda that she was disappointed in her purchase because the blouse had not held its color or shape and she wanted to return it. Linda listened carefully and took a second look at the blouse. She knew that Blackwells had not stocked this manufacturer for at least a year and therefore that the blouse had to have been purchased well beyond the 30 days return policy of the store. Linda asked the customer if she had the receipt, and the customer shook her head no. In her mind, Linda reviewed the company's policies and procedures for returned merchandise—articles must be returned within 30 days of purchase and with a receipt for a full refund.

5

Linda needed a minute to consider what she should do. She asked the customer to continue looking and said she would be back shortly. Linda was trying to decide if she could do anything about the used merchandise and if she required a supervisor's approval.

Recently Blackwells had initiated a new employee empowerment program in selected departments. Her department was one of the chosen areas and Linda had completed a series of seminars on making empowered decisions. Although Linda's first response was to call in a supervisor, she hesitated, remembering the program.

Linda returned to the customer and explained that most refunds required a receipt and that the merchandise be purchased within the last 30 days. She continued by mentioning that the store no longer carried that brand and had not done so for several months. However, Linda continued, Blackwells customers are valued beyond any single item. Would the customer consider a 50 percent discount on the blouse of her choice? Linda paused and smiled at the customer, not saying a word. The customer spoke next. "Yes, that would be fine. I probably have had the blouse over 30 days and I would like half off another blouse."

Linda completed the sale and thanked the customer for bringing the problem merchandise to her attention. As the customer left, Linda smiled, feeling satisfied with having made her first empowered decision. ■

Linda's experience shows how empowerment combines company policy and customer service. For a business to be successful, policy and service must match and complement each other. Both management and employees must understand and be committed to this important relationship. Employee empowerment programs go a long way toward ensuring the smooth connection between policy and service.

CONNECTING GOOD BUSINESS TO EMPOWERMENT

For a business to thrive, many diverse segments must meld together to form a cohesive and focused organization. Management, the employees, and the product or service all play an important part. Empowerment provides the opportunity for management to place many decisions and responsibilities in the hands of the employees. Empowered employees can provide streamlined service and offer solutions to customer problems that may, if not resolved, cost the business a sale and a customer.

Most companies want to increase sales and/or services by retaining current customers and acquiring new ones. Research concludes that 68 percent of the clients doing business with any one profitable company are repeat and referral customers. Research also suggests that the cost of attracting new business is five times greater than keeping current customers. If an empowered organization improves the quality of a product or service, the effects on the business can be very positive.

A top-notch management team with an insecure employee base will certainly struggle to keep customers. If management and employees are not working toward a common, well-communicated goal, they can't focus on maintaining a solid customer base, let alone build a new customer base.

MANAGEMENT'S ROLE

What is management's role in creating the best environment for employee empowerment and reaching company goals? Decisions relating to products (or services), pricing, advertising, merchandising, and hiring traditionally fall under management's responsibility. While policy is often determined at the top of an organization, actual customer contact is usually found between the employees and the customer.

If a product or service is poorly designed, poorly marketed, or poorly priced, it is not likely to sell, even with 100 of the country's best salespeople. But assuming that a desired product or service is offered and is effectively marketed and priced, having an empowered workforce lays a solid foundation for maintaining and building a strong customer base.

SIX KEY ISSUES FOR MANAGEMENT

If management is to forge a link between company policy, its product, and the customer, managers must build the necessary framework to ensure employee commitment to make it all work. An effective employee empowerment program can provide that link. Empowering employees to improve product quality, to improve the speed of customer response, and to quickly resolve problems (like Linda Pippen) can positively affect the success of the business.

For empowerment to work and to function smoothly, management needs to focus on six key issues:

1. Training.
2. Motivation.
3. Communication.
4. Effective listening.
5. Responding.
6. Self-analysis.

In the next sections, each of the six issues will be explored. Following the explanation of each issue and its part in making empowerment work, two profiles will be highlighted showing different approaches to the key issue. After reading the profiles consider this question: As a manager, do you think more like Rebecca or like Shanna?

SIX KEY ISSUES

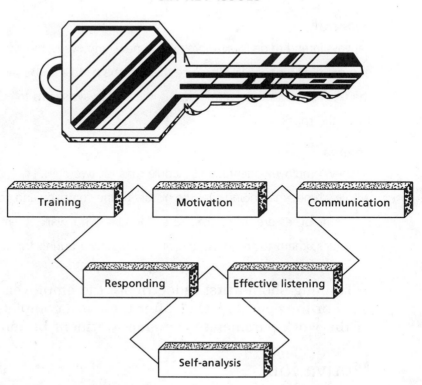

Training

For empowerment to work, employees have to understand their job and its responsibilities. Every employee deserves a thorough orientation program and complete training. Managers must allot sufficient time to prepare new hires for their duties and tutor current employees in new products or procedures. For empowerment to work, the employee needs to understand both his or her role in the organization and the job profile. An employee who is not secure in his or her position is not going to be able to make appropriate decisions that correspond to the organization's goals. Inadequate training puts the employee in a precarious position and does not create a comfortable platform from which to assume decision-making responsibilities.

Who Are You?

Rebecca

I always intend to dedicate more time to new employees, but there never seems to be enough time. I generally introduce them to the people in the same work area and let them take it from there. I'm lucky—someone always seems to adopt them and show them the ropes.

Shanna

My new employee orientation schedule runs for two days. I spend the first two hours with each new hire going over the history of the company and company policy. Next, new employees are introduced to a "buddy" who walks them through the plant, introduces them to the staff, and offers assistance during the first few days. ■

Training should first indoctrinate the employee about the company or the new skill. Only after there is a complete understanding of the work parameters can empowerment be initiated.

Motivation

As described in Chapter 3, money is not the true trigger of performance. It is management's responsibility to motivate the workforce to perform at peak level. An employee who does not care about the company or its product certainly won't care about its customers. Managers should attempt to discover their employees' "hot buttons" in order to create a solid work environment.

For an empowerment program to be effective, the extrinsic factors and the job environment must shape comfortable and safe surroundings, but the intrinsic factors must provide the stimulation for empowered employees to take risks in making their own decisions.

Refer back to your motivation profile developed in Chapter 3 (pages 39–40) to determine which factors and rewards may be motivating.

Who Are You?

Rebecca

I would like to spend at least 15 minutes once a month with each member of my group. I know it is important to find out what they like about their job and what their frustrations are; however, I find that months have gone by and I still have not had a talk with each one of them.

Shanna

The members of my group are required to personally stop by my office to pick up their paychecks. I make it a point to invite them to sit down and talk for a few minutes. The more I know about my staff and vice versa, the better we work as a team. ■

Communication

Open communication with all company employees is a key to establishing a successful employee empowerment program. The opposite philosophy of "telling them only what they need to know" is dangerous and unproductive. Allowing suspicion and uncertainty to gain hold through the grapevine results in distrust. Employees will not allow you to empower them with additional responsibilities and potential authority if they feel that the message being delivered is incomplete. Most employees will slip into a "CYB" (cover your back) mode of operation in order to protect themselves.

Who Are You?

Rebecca

I barely have time to keep informed myself. I attempted to hold staff meetings, but everyone complained that they were a waste of time. Half the time, my subordinates know what is happening before I do.

Shanna

Communication between me and my group of employees takes two forms. We hold brief department meetings every two weeks so that we get at least a little face-to-face

5

time with each other. Second, urgent information that surfaces between meetings is posted on several bulletin boards throughout the work area and in the lunch room and staff lounges. ■

Effective Listening

If you are a manager who considers your own viewpoint as the only correct one, you will never be able to instill empowerment in your employees.

Managers should stay tuned to employees. The issues and/or concerns brought to management by employees are important to *them*. Careful consideration of what is significant to all parties is an absolute key to the company's success. Keep in mind that hearing is not listening.

Who Are You?

Rebecca
I think I deserve every penny I earn just for putting up with all the verbal abuse I am surrounded by. Complaining employees seem to invade my time at least hourly. They expect me to remember each of their names and problems. What am I, a walking memory bank?

Shanna
I pride myself on knowing every employee by his or her first name. I make a conscious effort to remember each one's name by repeating it several times during a conversation. When one of my employees has a problem, I take note and really listen. ■

Listening is a learned skill that must be practiced. Just being born with two ears and one mouth does not make us a better listener than speaker. The following table lists four listening techniques and their purposes. Several examples for each technique are provided.

Technique	Purpose	Examples
Neutral encouraging	To convey interest and encourage the person to keep talking	"I see . . ." "Go on . . ." "Yes . . ."
Reflecting	To show understanding and acceptance of what the speaker is saying; to build rapport	"You feel that . . ." "Do you think . . ."
Asking questions	To get additional information and encourage further exploration	"How long have you felt like this?" "Was that the best way to . . . ?"
Feedback: paraphrasing and summarizing	To confirm meaning and show you understand what is being said	"As I understand it, you . . ."

5

Your Turn

Based on your current experience, provide your own examples of each technique.

1. Neutral encouraging   _____

    _____

2. Reflecting   _____

    _____

3. Asking questions   _____

    _____

4. Feedback   _____

    _____

By writing your own response examples, you will begin to understand that listening is a practiced skill. *How* you listen and *how well* you listen will determine whether your employees will open up to you and discuss their problems or concerns regarding the empowerment program. Empowerment is a two-way street. Both supervisors and employees must have a means to react and improve.

Responding

Responding quickly and following up consistently are essential skills for managers and empowered employees. Delayed decisions or slow delivery of crucial information causes frustration and anger in both customers and employees. Managers who are role models of quick response and decisive action find it easier to empower their employees to do the same. Research has found that a majority of people are willing to wait, as long as they feel some action is being taken and a resolution is forthcoming. It is when employees (or customers) believe that nothing is being done to help them and that no one cares about their problem that frustration takes over.

Who Are You?

Rebecca

I reserve one of my IN baskets for follow-up responses. It is a very full basket most days. I am afraid to sort through it and get to the bottom. I will probably find month-old (or older) responses still waiting. I have got to find a better system or get another secretary. After all, I am only one person.

Shanna

I finally have developed a faster, cleaner response system. I make decisions relating to staff time-off requests or customer merchandise complaints within 24 hours. For more difficult decisions, I set a time frame and note it on my calendar so that I don't forget to follow up. Even if I cannot respond immediately, employees or customers are contacted to keep them informed. ∎

Self-Analysis

The ability to analyze your own competence and to recognize that not every action you take or decision you make will be the right one is critical to initiating an employee empowerment schedule. Capable managers in successful companies realize that constant self-analysis (informal or formal) is necessary for growth and development of a company and its employees. Everyone errs in judgment on occasion.

Employees empowered with the authority to make decisions will also make mistakes. Training and follow-up can reduce the number of mistakes, but managers must give employees the opportunity to analyze their own misdirection and (with management's help) take corrective action. Employee empowerment depends on ongoing analysis and trust in employees to correct mistakes when necessary.

5

Who Are You?

Rebecca

I cannot understand why I keep having to replace staff. I know that I have the highest turnover in the company, but I can't help it if I set higher standards. Maybe I shouldn't worry about it. After all, the people who stick with me are the ones who want to be here, and those who can't make the grade should be out of here.

Shanna

Keeping the same group of employees is important to a cohesive department. We get to know each other and work as a team. On occasion, someone errs in judgment, including me, but by reviewing the incorrect decision, each of us gets a little smarter. I take each employee resignation or dismissal seriously. Did I make the wrong decision in hiring? Should I have provided more training? ■

■ Your Turn: Self-Analysis Test

The following is a checklist of personal characteristics important for supervisors involved in employee empowerment. Check the column that applies most frequently to you. Answer each question quickly.

Characteristic	Always	Sometimes	Rarely
Energetic	_____	_____	_____
Assertive	_____	_____	_____
Organized	_____	_____	_____
Cooperative	_____	_____	_____
Knowledgeable about technical matters	_____	_____	_____
Effective communicator	_____	_____	_____
Persistent	_____	_____	_____
Patient	_____	_____	_____
Able to set reachable standards	_____	_____	_____
Flexible	_____	_____	_____

■ **Score** ────────────────────────────────

Multiply each Always by 3, multiply each Sometimes by 2, and count each Rarely as 1.

Score	Meaning
30	Retake the test. No one is that perfect.
29–20	You have many of the qualities needed for a supervisor of an empowered group of employees.
19–11	You have the potential to develop into an effective supervisor of empowered employees. Review the checklist. Which characteristics do you score low on? Evaluate how to improve on these areas.
10	You have considerable work to do before an effective employee empowerment program can be implemented. The characteristics listed above are important to the success of empowerment. Consider each characteristic and how you can improve in each area.

MAKING A COMMITMENT

Making the initial commitment to begin an employee empowerment plan starts with management's decision that an empowered workforce will be good for the organization, for management, and for the employees.

As you have read in this book, implementing an empowerment program requires a thorough and honest evaluation of the organization's management style, the ability to identify the jobs best suited for empowerment, and an awareness that each employee is different in what inspires him or her to take risks and assume additional responsibilities.

For empowerment to work, managers must be willing to work through any obstacles and differences and must be prepared to handle employee reactions to the plan. A successful empowerment program doesn't just happen. It also requires a willingness to revise the program based on some trial and error and on the effects empowerment has on the employees. In Chapter 6, we will look at these effects.

5

Chapter 5
Checkpoints

✔ Managers and employees must work toward common, well-communicated company goals.

✔ Thorough training is management's first key issue in undertaking employee empowerment.

✔ It is management's responsibility to research the personal motivating factors for each employee.

✔ Open communication is an important key to maintaining employee empowerment.

✔ Managers must practice listening skills using paraphrasing, reflecting, and questioning techniques.

✔ Responding quickly and following up consistently are essential skills for managers and empowered employees.

6 | The Effects of Empowerment

This chapter will help you to: ————————

- See the connection between employee empowerment and productivity.
- Identify the effects of empowerment on employees.
- Consider the effects of empowerment on your customers.

Janet Stein walked into the board meeting carrying a cumbersome yet well-organized stack of papers. As she entered, she surveyed the group sitting around the oval table. One by one, the board members stopped talking as they noticed her arrival. Janet took her seat at the table.

"Well, good morning to all and thank you for attending the fiscal year-end meeting of Stein Computer and Software. Let me open the meeting by asking each of our three department heads for a synopsis of the year. Mr. McGillvry, as production manager, why don't you begin."

Mr. McGillvry briefly explained that the company's newly implemented employee empowerment program has started to show encouraging production numbers. As the various groups of production staff (assembly, packaging, shipping) had been empowered to develop their own work profiles and set production standards, the assembly section increased its output by 22 percent while packaging and shipping decreased their error margins to 8 percent.

6

Janet nodded slightly at Mr. McGillvry and turned to the human resources manager, Chris Mitchell. "Ms. Mitchell, could you update us on our employee resources?" Ms. Mitchell opened her notebook and began by giving the numbers of employees in each department, both full time and part-time. The numbers reflect a slight decrease from the previous year in total number of staff. However, there was a significant decrease in employee turnover. Since the employee empowerment program has been in effect, only 12 employees resigned their positions. Two moved out of town, two new mothers opted not to return to work, and three long-term employees retired, leaving five employees who could not adapt to new responsibilities. In fact, Ms. Mitchell added, the year-end HR survey indicated higher levels of self-esteem and increased confidence levels.

Janet Stein could not help smiling as she turned to the company's customer service supervisor, Mr. Qui Vranas. "Well, Mr. Vranas, what would you like to add to our fiscal year-end picture?" "I, too, can paint a rosy picture," began Qui. "Increased production has us delivering faster, and fewer errors in shipping, along with better packaging, has our complaint calls way down."

Employee empowerment appeared to have had positive effects across all departmental boundaries.

Thanking all the department heads, Janet Stein continued the meeting, "Well, ladies and gentleman of the board, if you will open your portfolios to the financial statement, I believe you will be able to see the positive results of employee empowerment in our positive financial figures." ∎

The scenario in the opening vignette shows the interplay of employee empowerment with production, customer service, and the employees themselves. All departments are affected by an empowerment program. The results of a properly implemented program can ripple through all areas and bring positive financial and human results.

Let's take a more detailed look at each of these three areas: productivity, employee relations, and customer service.

EMPLOYEE EMPOWERMENT

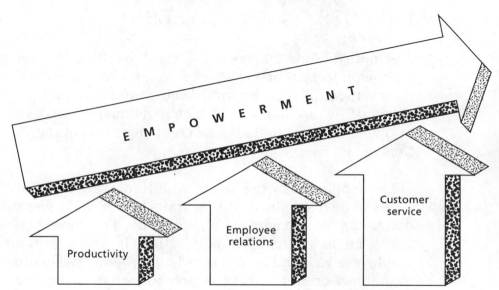

6

EFFECTS ON PRODUCTIVITY

Productivity is the easiest of all empowerment effects to measure. The number of computers, cases of soda, or orders received can be counted. When productivity increases, employees empowered to make decisions and choices that affect their own work and the organization begin to see the bigger picture of how what they do fits in to the success of the business. People are more satisfied and enthusiastic when they have the freedom to use their talents. Empowerment instills an individual sense of pride and accomplishment that spills over to benefit everyone.

Empowered supervisors actively involve their employees in planning and decision-making processes. They infuse mutual trust and develop collaborative goals. They set achievable goals and recognize accomplishments. The results are a more productive workforce that pushes through difficult challenges and reaches for innovative solutions.

EFFECTS ON EMPLOYEES

As employees assume greater control over their work environment and begin to self-direct work efforts, there is a natural increase in their self-confidence. Improved self-confidence leads to greater self-esteem. The development of such individual control creates a sense of ownership and initiative as creativity is encouraged and innovation recognized.

The employee of the 1990s is different from the worker of the 1950s or 1970s. Valued worker traits in the 1950s were conformity, obligation, permanence, and simplicity. Employees valued job security far more than job satisfaction. It was important for 1950s employees to blend in, not stand out. The overwhelming obligation to support one's family took precedence over any risk-taking.

The concept of employee empowerment would have had difficulty taking hold in the 1950s. Developing individual potential was not in the company's list of goals and objectives. Each worker had a role to play in the daily regime, but the work was to be done the same way every day. Only supervisors could suggest changes and potential improvements to senior managers. Front-line workers were not going to risk job security for a sense of ownership.

By the late 1970s, freedom and self-indulgence were values held by people entering the workforce, and so the nature of the workplace changed. Sometimes called the "me generation," people of the late 1970s entering the workforce sought individuality above all

else, and this self-centered look at life created a transient workforce. Workers of the late 1970s would change jobs frequently if job
expectations were not met or if restrictions squelched individual
freedom.

As in the 1950s, the concept of employee empowerment would
not have gained acceptance in the late 1970s, because although
empowerment is based on individual control and self-direction, the
overall objective is the betterment of the work team and the company. Innovation under employee empowerment never loses focus
on how an adjustment or change in one area will affect the results
in all areas. The 1970s worker may have sought to understand the
complexities of issues affecting his or her work environment but
cared more about how they affected him or her individually.

However, the 1990s work environment lends itself well to the
growth of empowerment programs. Today's employees, like those
in the 1970s, value individual style, but today's employees also value
accountability. Fulfillment is important to today's worker, but so is
feeling included as part of the company's decisions and goals.
Employee empowerment offers a sense of ownership that creates
energy and enthusiasm for the work being done as well as for the
company. The 1990s worker will assume the risks of self-direction
for the rewards of self-esteem.

Developing and maintaining employees' self-esteem is a crucial
factor in empowering employees. Self-esteem could be simply defined as "having a good opinion about oneself." People with high
self-esteem are confident about their abilities and excited about
exploring new opportunities.

In fostering self-esteem in employees, their feelings of self-worth
should be preserved. Their ideas and suggestions should be acknowledged, and confidence in their skills should be expressed.
They should be treated as intelligent, valuable members of the
organization.

As we learned in Chapter 5, listening skills are critical. Paying close attention to what someone says and responding to his or her comments shows value and respect of employees. Always be specific and concrete when praising an employee, as in these examples:

"I appreciate your organizing the warehouse inventory. Now we won't order unnecessary supplies and waste thousands of dollars."

"Your idea to reverse the door assembly process will shave 10 minutes off processing each piece. The time saved will allow us to complete 20 percent more product."

▌Think about It: Building Self-Esteem

This exercise will help you foster your employees' self-esteem. Be honest; there are no right or wrong answers. Which response would you give for each item below?

1. The survey results are on your desk. I finished them a week early.
   a. This is the first project you ever finished early.
   b. I'll take a look at them.
   c. Thank you. I appreciate the early finish. It will give me a little more time to write my report.
2. The copy machine is now up and running. I figured out what was wrong.
   a. It's about time. I hate that machine.
   b. Great, next time I'll know who to call.
   c. Thanks for taking the initiative to do that. I can get my report copied now.
3. If you would like help on research and writing that report, I would be interested. I did a school paper on the same subject.

    a. I'd prefer to do it myself.

    b. Sure, maybe I'll take you up on your offer.

    c. I would appreciate your input. Take a look at this first draft and tell me what you think.

4. It is impossible to get my payroll report in by noon. I am always late because of our flexible work schedule.

    a. You had better figure out a way to get it here on time.

    b. You are not alone, but please try harder.

    c. The other three departments on flex time have voiced similar concerns. Why don't the four of you get together and work on a solution?

Now that you have completed the exercise, look back once more. The **a** answers are the least appropriate for maintaining self-esteem; the **c** answers are more specific and positive.

6

■ Your Turn

Write a poor response to each statement and then a better response. Be aware of the difference between short, abrupt responses and specific ones that do not damage the confidence or self-worth of your employees.

1. What an earful I just got. Some customer ripped me apart about not delivering her furniture on time. Like it's my fault.

_____

_____

_____

_____

_____

_____

2. I know I agreed to work this Saturday, but my daughter's soccer team made the finals and I have to drive the team van.

_____

_____

_____

_____

_____

_____

3. I just wrote a computer program that will cut our accounting time in half.

_____

_____

_____

_____

_____

_____

EFFECTS ON CUSTOMER SERVICE

Without customers, a company will not stay in business. One of the goals of business is to acquire new customers, retain them, and have them consume more and more of the company's products and services. Companies that have become legends in customer service create flexible policies. Empowered employees can make decisions that fulfill customer needs and can make exceptions that solve problems.

Customer service research has found that only very few disgruntled buyers will bother to tell the company about their dissatisfaction. The few who do speak up represent a valuable opportunity. Customers who receive assistance and a satisfactory end result to their complaint will do business again with the company 96 percent of the time. Not only will they buy the product or service again, but they will tell their story to friends and acquaintances who in turn are more likely to try the company's product or service. Consumers will continue to frequent businesses that are responsive to their needs.

As mentioned in Chapter 5, business experts state that 68 percent of any business must be repeat or referral based if the company is to be successful. Advertising for new customers is five times more costly than keeping a repeat customer buying again and again.

How does empowerment improve customer service?

- Empowered employees are able to resolve customer problems more quickly.
- Creating solutions for customers with problems is reduced to one or two decision layers, not many.
- The time saved in resolving customer problems quickly allows more time for creating new sales.
- A reputation for exemplary customer service extends beyond current customers and begins to create new customers as the word spreads about the company's quick, responsive actions.

In Chapter 7, we will highlight two companies that have done just this. The case studies reflect the positive effects that Mary Kay Cosmetics and the Ritz-Carlton Hotel Company, L.L.C. have produced as a result of employee empowerment. Each has developed an empowered employee base that has resulted in improved productivity, a more confident employee workforce, and a loyal following of customers.

6

Chapter 6
Checkpoints

✔ Empowerment instills an individual sense of pride in accomplishments and bolsters productivity standards.

✔ Empowerment allows employees to assume greater control over their work environment, and self-directed work efforts build greater self-confidence.

✔ Empowerment affects customer service by permitting employees to solve customer problems quickly.

7 | Employee Empowerment in Action

Throughout this book you have read about employee motivation, key management issues, and how to develop standards. You have been asked to take self-analysis tests and to create job profiles as well as to identify extrinsic and intrinsic job factors. This final chapter presents two case studies demonstrating employee empowerment at work.

Each case study highlights key points of employee empowerment. The first one follows the traditional employee/supervisor/management business model using The Ritz-Carlton Hotel Company, L.L.C., as the example. The second case study features the direct sales industry, where company growth and success rely on a team of independent salespeople, Mary Kay Cosmetics, Inc.

CASE STUDY 1: THE RITZ-CARLTON® HOTEL COMPANY, L.L.C.

The Ritz-Carlton Hotel Company, L.L.C., is the only hotel chain ever to have won the prestigious Malcolm Baldrige National Quality Award, an award that signifies the highest level of total quality management (TQM). The road to winning the award in 1992 was a difficult one for the company and required every employee to buy in to the process of TQM.

Total Quality Management

Total Quality Management, often referred to as TQM, is an organizational management concept that strives for perfection in all phases of customer/company contact. TQM encompasses improving the product, as well as its manufacture, delivery, and service. When TQM is properly incorporated, company executives, supervisors, and employees strive for reliability and consistency that ensures satisfied customers at every level of the distribution cycle.

Horst Schulze, president and chief operating officer, admits that he was not an immediate convert to the principles of TQM. Realizing back in 1987 that not every Ritz-Carlton customer was a satisfied guest, Schulze decided that steps needed to be taken to reduce errors that reflected poorly on guest services. According to Schulze, a lot of mistakes were being made. Guest check-in was too slow, messages were not always delivered on a timely basis, and occasionally a room would not be immaculately clean. However, Ritz-Carlton management felt that these mistakes were not to be blamed on individual employees, but were instead caused by breakdowns in the internal systems. By reevaluating the system and incorporating total quality management, the customers, the company, and the employees all came out ahead.

The results of the program have been impressive, but the goal to achieve an even higher standard sits on the desk of Horst Shulze. The sign he keeps on his desk reads "Six Sigma." It is a mathematical term that means zero defects.

Issue: Overmanagement

"You know the three obstacles to TQM?" asks Schulze. "Top management, middle management, and lower management." As we saw in Chapter 2, overmanagement was one of three common obstacles to empowering employees. Micromanaging creates a limited step-by-step work environment where employees wait for the next instruction. Overmanagement reduces individual initiative and blankets employee self-confidence. When employees are empowered to react to problems and customer requests, they feel more a part of the organization; they feel like contributors.

In order to solidify the concept that everyone can contribute to the organization, Ritz-Carlton employees carry a small tri-fold card with them at all times. In a pocket of every uniform, this laminated reminder states the credo of the company, the "Three Steps of Service" for every employee, and the 20 "Ritz-Carlton Basics" to both customer and employee satisfaction. Step 20 reads, "Protecting the assets of a Ritz-Carlton Hotel is the responsibility of every employee."

THE RITZ-CARLTON BASICS

1. The Credo will be known, owned, and energized by all employees.
2. Our motto is: "We are Ladies and Gentlemen serving Ladies and Gentlemen." Practice teamwork and "lateral service" to create a positive work environment.
3. The three steps of service shall be practiced by all employees.
4. All employees will successfully complete Training Certification to ensure they understand how to perform to the Ritz-Carlton standards in their position.
5. Each employee will understand their work area and Hotel goals as established in each strategic plan.
6. All employees will know the needs of their internal and external customers (guests and employees) so that we may deliver the products and services they expect. Use guest preference pads to record specific needs.
7. Each employee will continuously identify defects (Mr. BIV) throughout the Hotel.
8. Any employee who receives a customer complaint "owns" the complaint.
9. Instant guest pacification will be ensured by all. React quickly to correct the problem immediately. Follow up with a telephone call within 20 minutes to verify the problem has been resolved to the customer's satisfaction. Do everything you possibly can to never lose a guest.
10. Guest incident action forms are used to record and communicate every incident of guest dissatisfaction. Every employee is empowered to resolve the problem and to prevent a repeat occurrence.
11. Uncompromising levels of cleanliness are the responsibility of every employee.
12. "Smile—We are on stage." Always maintain positive eye contact. Use the proper vocabulary with our guests. (Use words like—"Good Morning," "Certainly," "I'll be happy to," and "My pleasure.")

(Continued)

13. Be an ambassador of your Hotel in and outside of the work place. Always talk positively. No negative comments.

14. Escort guests rather than pointing out directions to another area of the Hotel.

15. Be knowledgeable of Hotel information (hours of operation, etc.) to answer guest inquiries. Always recommend the Hotel's retail and food and beverage outlets prior to outside facilities.

16. Use proper telephone etiquette. Answer within three rings and with a "smile." When necessary, ask the caller, "May I place you on hold." Do not screen calls. Eliminate call transfers when possible.

17. Uniforms are to be immaculate. Wear proper and safe footwear (clean and polished), and your name tag. Take pride and care in your personal appearance (adhering to all grooming standards).

18. Ensure all employees know their roles during emergency situations and are aware of fire and life safety response processes.

19. Notify your supervisor immediately of hazards, injuries, equipment or assistance that you need. Practice energy conservation and proper maintenance and repair of Hotel property and equipment.

20. Protecting the assets of a Ritz-Carlton Hotel is the responsibility of every employee.

THREE STEPS OF SERVICE

1
A warm and sincere greeting. Use the guest name, if and when possible.

2
Anticipation and compliance with guest needs.

3
Fond farewell. Give them a warm good-bye and use their names, if and when possible.

"We Are Ladies and Gentlemen Serving Ladies and Gentlemen."

THE RITZ-CARLTON

CREDO

The Ritz-Carlton Hotel is a place where the genuine care and comfort of our guests is our highest mission.

We pledge to provide the finest personal service and facilities for our guests who will always enjoy a warm, relaxed yet refined ambience.

The Ritz-Carlton experience enlivens the senses, instills well-being, and fulfills even the unexpressed wishes and needs of our guests.

Recall the definition of employee empowerment in Chapter 1: "Empowerment is the ability to let others assume the responsibilities, risks, and rewards associated with making their own decisions."

Issue: The Effects of Empowerment

The early dividends of the Ritz-Carlton TQM program have been most apparent in two areas: customer satisfaction and employee morale. In addition, the reduction in mistakes has reduced the number of times the properties have had to make adjustments to guests, thereby decreasing expenses while increasing employee productivity. These results are similar to the ones discussed in Chapter 6. The effects of empowerment are most clearly defined in the areas of productivity, employee relations, and customer service.

Productivity. Productivity improvements have been a team effort at Ritz-Carlton. For example, a recent project to increase the life span of guest towels involved managers, supervisors, housekeeping staff, and laundry personnel. The team created for the project has been empowered to develop a solution that will first be implemented at one property and later at all Ritz-Carlton hotels. As we saw in Chapter 6, employees empowered to make decisions and choices that affect their own work and the organization begin to see the bigger picture of how what they do fits in to the success of the organization.

Employee Relations. Prior to TQM, Ritz-Carlton's annual employee turnover rate was 90 percent. This high rate of replacing employees was costly in both money and time. Ritz-Carlton estimated that the financial investment to recruit and train each new employee was about $5,000 per individual hired. TQM is credited with reducing that turnover rate to 30 percent a year. Keeping employees longer at Ritz-Carlton hotels begins with a thorough orientation process. Candidates for employment may go through four interviews before being offered a position, and every new employee attends a two-day classroom orientation that drills in the company's credo, mission statement, and business philosophy. The company philosophy and motto, "Ladies and Gentlemen serving Ladies and Gentlemen," is repeated over and over from the office of Horst Schulze to the valet parking attendant. After 21 days, each new employee is required to attend an orientation class reunion that encourages feedback on the first three weeks at a Ritz-Carlton hotel.

Customer Service.   Customer service at Ritz-Carlton properties is quickly becoming a standard for the industry. Each employee at every level is offered the opportunity to fix any and all guest problems. Guest requests or complaints are immediately "owned" by the employee to whom the request or complaint was made. Ownership of the problem empowers the employee to do whatever it takes to resolve the issue.

Even giving directions to the pool becomes "owned." Guests are never simply given directions, but instead are escorted to their destination by the employee, regardless of whether the guest stopped the general manager or the room attendant. The decision to empower each employee to fix every complaint has resulted in an increase in individual pride and accomplishment, which has translated into a more enthusiastic and satisfied workforce and a more loyal client base.

Issue: Feedback

Feedback is an essential element in every empowerment program. Chapter 2 listed the guidelines: Feedback must be (1) timely, (2) balanced, (3) specific, (4) objective, and (5) positive. At Ritz-Carlton hotels, various departments gather for daily "line-up." These brief group meetings can be in a hallway, employee lounge, or other designated area. "Line-up" is designed to give supervisors an opportunity to relay new information, discuss problem areas, and run down the day's work activities. This pep talk also affords the opportunity for recognition, encouragement, and positive direction. Employees are encouraged to communicate their problem areas, relate a guest satisfaction story, or offer a comment or suggestion to the supervisor's remarks. "Line-up" ensures fewer misunderstandings and keeps communication between employees and supervisors on a two-way path.

A second way of gathering feedback is the "good idea board." On this board, employees can place an idea for improving hotel standards or eliminating waste—or any other idea that just sounds good. Supervisors review the ideas, taking many through an adoption process. This process incorporates the idea into Ritz-Carlton's policies, recognizes the employee who created the idea, and often involves the employee on the development team. Prizes are awarded on a regular basis for the very best ideas on the good idea board.

The Ritz-Carlton Hotel Company, L.L.C., has merged a traditional management model with an employee empowerment program that is proving successful for the organization and its customers. Each employee contributes to the operation of the hotel and plays a vital role in the overall experience of each guest. Perhaps Ritz-Carlton's Basic 6 says it best: "All employees will know the needs of their internal and external customers (guests and employees) so that we may deliver the products and services they expect."

CASE STUDY 2: MARY KAY COSMETICS, INC.

Mary Kay Ash founded Mary Kay Cosmetics in 1963 as a "dream company" offering women the opportunity for financial independence, career advancement, and personal fulfillment. A pioneer in the direct-sales industry, the company has grown from a small business to the largest direct seller of skin-care products in the United States, with more than 350,000 independent consultants in 23 countries worldwide.

The management structure of Mary Kay Cosmetics was designed to allow outward growth, not upward mobility. There is no corporate ladder to climb; advancement along a career path builds on each succeeding layer. Every new associate starts as a beauty consultant and can earn her way to team manager and up to national sales director. At every level of the organization, each person is empowered to control her own business growth while encouraging the development of personal recruits. In essence, the company systematically empowers each level to empower the next level.

Issue: Job Environment versus Job Content

What is unique in the Mary Kay Cosmetics empowerment program is the absence of the usual *job environment factors* found in traditional management structures. As discussed in Chapter 3, the five main facets of job environment are (1) policy and administration, (2) compensation, (3) working conditions, (4) manager/employee relations, and (5) peer relations.

While the Mary Kay organization establishes a framework for job environment, it allows individuals more freedom of choice.

For example, most company policy manuals set forth the regulations for overtime and sick leave, but not at Mary Kay Cosmetics. Every sales consultant, from new recruits to national sales directors, works as many or as few hours as she chooses. In the area of compensation, the direct sales format ensures that there are not limits on pay. Commissions are paid on products sold and on the sales of the unit. The amount of income obtained by any member of the sales force is directly related to individual effort. The same is true for working conditions, since each consultant arranges for her own space and furnishings.

One job environment factor that is in place at Mary Kay is manager/employee relations (in this case, leader/recruit relations) and peer relations. Team leaders provide instruction on product demonstrations, help set new recruit goals, and offer encouragement. According to Mary Kay Ash, "Not only do we teach our consultants how to set goals, we show them how to achieve those goals." Weekly team meetings tender support and build self-esteem among peers.

As we learned in Chapter 3, employee empowerment's success relies heavily on the *job content factors* of achievement, recognition, the work itself, responsibility, advancement, and growth/learning. The very essence of empowerment is encouraging a greater control of individual work effort, making decisions, and staying with projects through completion.

At every level of Mary Kay Cosmetics, these critical job content factors are at work. In her book, *Mary Kay on People Management*, Ms. Ash writes about an invisible sign that everyone wears. This sign says MAKE ME FEEL IMPORTANT because all of us want to feel good about ourselves. Recognition and reward are important aspects of this special message. Beginning with the "Pearls of Sharing" necklace offered to new recruits who share the Mary Kay business opportunity within their first month, to the pink Cadillacs that have become a signature trademark, every consultant is recognized at each level of achievement.

Issue: Management's Commitment to Empowerment

For employee empowerment to work in any organization, there must be a companywide commitment to the program. Management must recognize the six key issues that link policy to the end user: the customer. In Chapter 5, we saw how these issues lay the groundwork for ensuring employee commitment to company goals that result in customer satisfaction. To repeat, these issues are (1) training, (2) motivation, (3) communication, (4) effective listening, (5) responding, and (6) self-analysis.

    At Mary Kay, beauty consultants receive regular sales training and new-product training. *Training* may occur at monthly team meetings or at regional company-sponsored events. Understanding the products and their proper usage is important to both the individual consultant and to the Mary Kay organization. For Mary Kay, there are two equally important sets of customers. Each consultant is a Mary Kay customer and each product user is a customer. A long-built reputation for reliability and quality is maintained through the training processes, as is increased levels of self-esteem for each consultant. Once empowered with the knowledge of the products, and the self-confidence to demonstrate them, beauty consultants are encouraged to develop a customer base and to offer the Mary Kay system to other potential consultants.

    Motivation is an internal mechanism depending on what each person considers motivational. We discussed in Chapter 3 the fact that money is not necessarily a motivator. What inspired Mary Kay to start her organization was the desire to accomplish more after her first retirement. Using the Golden Rule as her guiding philosophy, she encourages the sales force to set priorities and make opportunities happen.

    Communication became the foundation for Mary Kay's "We Heard You" program. As a believer that people will support what they help to create, Mary Kay incorporates suggestions through a systematic method of analyzing the technical and procedural applicability of the suggestion, testing it, and communicating the results to the general body of associates. By enlisting the support of everyone involved, changes are easier to implement and overall self-esteem is raised. Open communication is a key to establishing a successful empowerment program.

    In her book, *Mary Kay on People Management*, Mary Kay Ash devotes a chapter to the art of listening. *Listening*, she states, is the most undervalued of all communication skills. It is an art that starts with undivided attention and can be an invaluable resource for ideas. Refer back to Chapter 5 for examples of listening techniques and their purpose.

At Mary Kay Cosmetics, an open door is the most important step in *responding* to the needs of all the company's customers, both internal and external. Giving a timely response is an essential skill both for managers and empowered employees. Open doors allow managers to get to know people. When managers help others get what they want, they naturally achieve their own goals. Unlike many traditional management structures, there are no titles on the doors at Mary Kay Cosmetics headquarters.

The last key issue discussed in Chapter 5 is *self-analysis*. For an organization to be successful, it must periodically take a close look at itself. Taking risks will mean making mistakes. Empowered team members with the authority to make decisions will not always make correct choices, but mistakes along the way can encourage personal growth and creativity. In a career no one ever stands still. All members of the Mary Kay organization must continually improve their skills in a lifetime self-improvement program.

A FINAL WORD

Employee empowerment can be a win-win experience for any company, its employees, and its customers. The customer gains in improved services, quality products, and a quick response to occasional problems. Employees gain increased self-esteem and self-confidence as they assume greater responsibilities, take risks, and become an important, integrated part of the organization. The company gains a faster and more efficient operation in which decisions are made promptly, products are continually improved, and the workforce stays on and grows along with the company.

Both Ritz-Carlton and Mary Kay have found empowering their workforces to be productive and rewarding. Employees who contribute to the decisions made within an organization build on the personal ownership they feel toward the company. People will support what they help create.

7

Post-Test

Congratulations on completing *Empowering Employees*. Complete the following assessment on implementing an employee empowerment program. How did you do?

	Always	Sometimes	Never
1. I involve others in planning the actions we will take.	_____	_____	_____
2. I take time to celebrate accomplishments as projects are completed.	_____	_____	_____
3. I make sure that employees understand projects and know what the end results should be.	_____	_____	_____
4. I give my employees the discretion to make their own decisions.	_____	_____	_____
5. I am open to suggestions on new ways of doing things.	_____	_____	_____
6. I show my appreciation for work well done.	_____	_____	_____
7. I ask "What can we learn?" when things go wrong.	_____	_____	_____

(Continued)

	Always	Sometimes	Never
8. I am willing to take risks, and I encourage my employees to do so.	_____	_____	_____
9. I consistently treat each member of my group with equal confidence and respect.	_____	_____	_____
10. I feel comfortable letting my employees make decisions.	_____	_____	_____
11. When implementing a new idea or project, I am careful to include my employees.	_____	_____	_____
12. I am willing to try a new procedure suggested by an employee even if I doubt the outcome.	_____	_____	_____
13. I make a conscious effort to recognize the work efforts of my employees.	_____	_____	_____
14. I believe that letting employees "own" a project is best for the company and the employee.	_____	_____	_____
15. I believe that empowered employees gain in self-confidence and self-esteem.	_____	_____	_____

Scoring

To find your score, count each Always as 3 points, each Sometimes as 2 points, and each Never as 1 point.

40 or higher

You will be successful in implementing an employee empowerment program.

32–39

You have most of the critical skills needed. Go back and evaluate your Sometimes and Never responses. What areas need improvement?

25–31

It is possible for you to implement a successful employee empowerment program. However, you are likely to struggle because some skills are missing. Go back and evaluate your Sometimes and Never responses. What areas need improvement?

24 and below

You have a difficult time letting go and letting others assume control. For employee empowerment to work, the employee must have a sense of ownership in the work. Go back and evaluate your Sometimes and Never responses. What areas need improvement?

Business Skills Express Series

This growing series of books addresses a broad range of key business skills and topics to meet the needs of employees, human resource departments, and training consultants.

To obtain information about these and other Business Skills Express books, please call Irwin Professional Publishing toll free at 1–800–634–3966.

Effective Performance Management
ISBN 1-55623-867-3

Hiring the Best
ISBN 1-55623-865-7

Writing that Works
ISBN 1-55623-856-8

Customer Service Excellence
ISBN 1-55623-969-6

Writing for Business Results
ISBN 1-55623-854-1

Powerful Presentation Skills
ISBN 1-55623-870-3

Meetings that Work
ISBN 1-55623-866-5

Effective Teamwork
ISBN 1-55623-880-0

Time Management
ISBN 1-55623-888-6

Assertiveness Skills
ISBN 1-55623-857-6

Motivation at Work
ISBN 1-55623-868-1

Overcoming Anxiety at Work
ISBN 1-55623-869-X

Positive Politics at Work
ISBN 1-55623-879-7

Telephone Skills at Work
ISBN 1-55623-858-4

Managing Conflict at Work
ISBN 1-55623-890-8

The New Supervisor: Skills for Success
ISBN 1-55623-762-6

The *Americans with Disabilities Act:* What Supervisors Need to Know
ISBN 1-55623-889-4

Managing the Demands of Work and Home
ISBN 0-7863-0221-6

Effective Listening Skills
ISBN 0-7863-0102-4

Goal Management at Work
ISBN 0-7863-0225-9

Positive Attitudes at Work
ISBN 0-7863-0100-8

Supervising the Difficult Employee
ISBN 0-7863-0219-4

Cultural Diversity in the Workplace
ISBN 0-7863-0125-2

Managing Change in the Workplace
ISBN 0-7863-0162-7

Negotiating for Business Results
ISBN 0-7863-0114-7

Practical Business Communication
ISBN 0-7863-0227-5

High Performance Speaking
ISBN 0-7863-0222-4

Delegation Skills
ISBN 0-7863-0105-9

**Coaching Skills: A Guide
for Supervisors**
ISBN 0-7863-0220-8

**Customer Service and
the Telephone**
ISBN 0-7863-0224-0

Creativity at Work
ISBN 0-7863-0223-2

**Effective Interpersonal
Relationships**
ISBN 0-7863-0255-0

The Participative Leader
ISBN 0-7863-0252-6

Building Customer Loyalty
ISBN 0-7863-0253-4

Getting and Staying Organized
ISBN 0-7863-0254-2

Business Etiquette
ISBN 0-7863-0323-9

Empowering Employees
ISBN 0-7863-0314-X

Training Skills for Supervisors
ISBN 0-7863-0313-1

Moving Meetings
ISBN 0-7863-0333-6

Multicultural Customer Service
ISBN 0-7863-0332-8